CRAZY LOVE

**More Than 200
Insanely Creative Ways
to Show Love**

Grace Edwards

Adamsmedia
Avon, Massachusetts

Published by
Adams Media, a division of F+W Media, Inc.
57 Littlefield Street, Avon, MA 02322. U.S.A.
www.adamsmedia.com

ISBN 10: 1-4405-5484-6
ISBN 13: 978-1-4405-5484-1
eISBN 10: 1-4405-5485-4
eISBN 13: 978-1-4405-5485-8

Printed in the United States of America.

10 9 8 7 6 5 4 3 2 1

Library of Congress Cataloging-in-Publication Data
Edwards, Grace.
  Crazy love / Grace Edwards.
    p. cm.
  ISBN 978-1-4405-5484-1 (pbk.) — ISBN 1-4405-5484-6 (pbk.) — ISBN 978-1-4405-
5485-8 (ebook) — ISBN 1-4405-5485-4 (ebook)
 1. Courtship. 2. Love. 3. Romanticism. I. Title.
 HQ801.E359 2012
 306.73'4—dc23
                          2012030103

This publication is designed to provide accurate and authoritative information with regard to
the subject matter covered. It is sold with the understanding that the publisher is not engaged
in rendering legal, accounting, or other professional advice. If legal advice or other expert
assistance is required, the services of a competent professional person should be sought.
    —From a *Declaration of Principles* jointly adopted by a Committee of the American Bar
                          Association and a Committee of Publishers and Associations

This book is available at quantity discounts for bulk purchases.
For information, please call 1-800-289-0963.

DEDICATION

This book is dedicated to lovers and romantics everywhere!

ACKNOWLEDGMENTS

To the team at Adams Media, for their continued hard work!

INTRODUCTION

It may be true that love is all you need, but how can you keep love fresh, creative, exciting, and romantic over the course of months or years? Sometimes it seems like there are really only a handful of romantic activities to choose from, and we all know what they are: a love note; a dinner date; a movie; a nice picnic. They're all fine, but they've all been done before, and it can be easy to get into a love rut by doing the same things over and over again. *Crazy Love* is here to change that! The ideas in this book will help you overcome the boring and ordinary, and set you on a course for adventure into uncharted territory. Some of the ideas presented here are unique twists and creative additions to the standard romance repertoire, while others are completely novel. Your partner will wonder just how you managed to come up with something so creative!

You can and should use this book in the way that suits you best: use the ideas as inspiration, and tweak them to meet your budget or time constraints, or follow them to the letter for a truly remarkable romantic experience. You know your relationship better than anyone else ever could, so use this knowledge to help you decide whether or not a particular romantic idea would excite your significant other. After all, some people are mortified by public displays of affection, while others can't get enough of them. Respect the needs and wishes of your partner, and you'll find that these ideas will take your relationship to a new level of romance that you have to feel to believe!

Write a song about her, and then hire a local band to play it for her. There are plenty of eager musicians in college music departments looking for quick gigs.

Get a fancy restaurant
to surprise him with his
favorite food, even though it's
not on the menu. Ask the kitchen
ahead of time, but be prepared
to try several places before
you find one that will do this
for you. It might help if you first
approached a smaller restaurant
that the two of you have
frequented previously, and where
you might be recognized.

Buy him a book he's been wanting to read, then paste a love letter on the inside back cover, so it's the last thing he sees.

Rent a billboard declaring your love on a road she drives every day. If that's well outside of your budget, you can hang a sign on an overpass.

Put love notes in your partner's books or magazines, so that she will find them when she least expects it. This works especially well if she is taking the magazine with her somewhere—to work or on a trip, for example.

Take a picture of the two of you, and then use photo editing software to place your faces on a backdrop derived from your partner's dream vacation location. If she always wanted to go to Venice, paste your heads in front of the canals of Venice. Have the photo made into a puzzle (there are several companies that do this) and when she's finished putting it together, surprise her with tickets to the destination in the puzzle!

Name a star after him
through the International
Star Registry, and then
go one step further: Buy
a telescope, and set it so
that it's focused on your
partner's star before he
comes home in the evening.
Bring him outside with
some wine and let him have
a look!

Video record yourself talking about all the things you love about her, and then ask your local movie theater to air it as a "preview" at a movie you take her to see.

• • •

Take him to a sports game, even a local high school or college game, and have the cheerleaders do a cheer of his name.

uy a dozen roses, and use them to design a scavenger hunt for her! Leave one rose on her car at work, along with a clue that will lead her to the next rose. Each subsequent rose is paired with a clue, until you ultimately lead her to a restaurant where you're already waiting.

Plan a complete surprise vacation for him: Pack his suitcase, call his boss to arrange his time off, and let his friends know what you're up to, as long as you trust them not to tell! On the day you leave, pack the luggage in secret, tell your partner you're taking him out to dinner, and then drive straight to the airport!

Hire a local artist to make a mixed-media collage, sculpture, or painting of the two of you, using some of your favorite photographs. If you don't have enough photos yet to pull this off, stage a quick photoshoot with a friend or a photographer to help round out the choices.

Plan a full-out surprise party for him on the anniversary of some small success or accomplishment, such as his one-year anniversary of when he learned to ski. Get him a cake, a card, and a small gift that relates to the anniversary in some way.

Surprise her by transforming your home into a spa, complete with a private masseuse (either you or an actual professional), soothing music, and a new bathrobe.

• • •

Put together a "tour" of his favorite movie or TV show. Go and visit the places where it was filmed, eat where and what the characters eat, and take pictures of yourselves in front of some of the recognizable landmarks.

Go for a picnic . . . during a workday! Buy all of the supplies you need, and then head out to his workplace for lunchtime. Give him a call or a text, and ask him to come outside. Then, use his lunch break to have a quick meal for the two of you! If there are parks around, go there; but if not, your car will do just fine.

Gather up any love letters
or cards the two of you
have exchanged, and have
them bound into a book
for safekeeping. There are
numerous options you
could take with the binding,
whether you prefer a
classical, leather-bound
volume, or something a bit
more contemporary.

Give her a locket with a meaningful picture in it. Each day, write a new small message and place it in the locket before she goes to work.

Buy ad space in the newspaper or magazine he reads, declaring your love for him. It might make sense not to use his real name, but make sure the message is still recognizably to him and from you.

Make a time capsule for your future selves. Seal photos, objects, and written memories from the year in a small storage container, put it away, and then open it up at a predetermined time with your partner. You can open this time capsule after your wedding, during an anniversary, on a birthday, or any day that you agree on!

Have a campout indoors. Use the stovetop to cook s'mores and hot dogs, lie out on an air mattress in the living room, and watch a fake fireplace DVD to set the campfire mood. Swap ghost stories, or just relax together with your "fire" and some s'mores.

Create a visual depiction of your relationship by collecting photos of the two of you that express what you love about your life together. Assemble them in a digital scrapbook and have a nice print edition made for an in-person gift.

Design an infographic that traces your lives before and after you met. It could be a complicated flow chart, a pictorial timeline, or something else entirely. You could even use it to pop a big question about the next stage of your life together!

Cultivate a new breed of roses and name it after her. Though this may sound like a difficult task, it only takes one or two growing seasons, and instructions can be found online.

Take a day off of work, and use the time to plant a small garden with all of her favorite plants.

Watch the sun rise and set on two different coasts. Travel first to the East Coast, and surprise her in the early morning with a breakfast picnic while the sun rises. Then, hop a flight to the West Coast, and head to a beach to watch the sun set over the Pacific.

For the social media—savvy partner, make an online "scrapbook" of your relationship by collecting old Facebook updates, tweets, blog posts, and photos that pertain to your relationship. Create a single online document, and then send it to her at the end of a long week for a sweet surprise.

Surprise her by arranging for her out-of-state family or friends to come visit for her birthday.

• • •

Buy his favorite book, whether it's a novel, poetry, or nonfiction, and take turns reading it aloud to each other, one chapter or poem at a time.

Give her a calendar for the upcoming year, marked with several "Mystery Dates" each month. When each of those days rolls around, take her on a fun and unique date! She'll love looking forward to the next "date" on her calendar. Try to vary the type of dates that you go on—the juxtaposition of the planned days with the unpredictability of the actual activity is what makes this fun.

Make a playlist on your smartphone of all of his favorite songs, and leave it inconspicuously in his car before he goes to work. Call your phone so that he realizes it's in the car with him, and then tell him to listen to the playlist. If you want, you can be more sensual with this too. Instead of just using his favorite songs, use some sexy songs that will get his mind working during the day.

*T*ake a vacation to a romantic hotel, and book one (or more) of their honeymoon packages — even if it's not your honeymoon! The two of you can have fun coming up with a backstory for your adventure, either using your own wedding history or making up what you'd like your wedding to be.

It may be out of your budget to buy a boat and name it after her, but how about buying a canoe or a kayak, and then painting her name on it? You can use the boat any time you go camping, paddling, or rafting, and it will be sure to be a conversation starter among friends, relatives, and neighbors.

Donate a wooden bench to your town in her name. Request that the bench be placed in a town park or common. Visit "her" bench once a month for a quick picnic or just to share some time there. There's something very romantic about being philanthropic together, and it's even better if the two of you can revisit the results of your philanthropy time and time again.

You may already know how to make his favorite dinner, but how about learning how to make his favorite candy at home? The Internet abounds with numerous copycat recipes for every kind of popular candy. Nothing surprises like homemade candy!

Pay for him to take a cooking class that's focused on a type of cuisine that he enjoys. At the conclusion of the class, schedule a quick trip to that country or region to try some of the food in person!

Write a book—and dedicate it to her. You can usually set up small book signings at local bookstores, even if your book is self-published. At your first book signing, invite her to sign a few, select limited editions along with you.

Take a scuba-diving class together!
As long as she's not afraid of the
water and can swim reasonably well,
scuba diving is a fantastic recreational
activity to learn together. When
you graduate the class, celebrate
by booking a quick getaway to a
Caribbean island—the ultimate scuba-
diving paradise—where the two of you
can practice the skills you've learned!
Even better, surprise her with the trip
directly after the last day of class—
have her bags packed ahead of time,
and head straight for the airport!

While he is at work, hire a professional sculptor to come to your residence and make a small sculpture. It can be a literal or figurative design, whichever you think he'll prefer. Have it made by the front door so he'll see it when he comes home!

Make an official-looking PowerPoint presentation detailing how much you love and care for her, and then send it to her work e-mail (from an e-mail account other than the one she usually gets from you) under a generic, business-y name. When she opens it, expecting business facts and figures, she'll get a nice surprise instead.

Buy her a vanity license plate that expresses your love! Make it even better by taking care of all of the paperwork, so that she isn't left with a headache when you give her the new plate.

Hire a videographer to follow the two of you around for an anniversary dinner, or even for a random dinner date. Ask them to try to capture the little moments between the two of you.

Keep a joint diary. At the end of each day, each of you take some time to write down any loving thoughts you've had during the day. Keep the pages separate, and show each other what you've written once a month (or once a week, if you prefer)!

Make your own drive-in movie theater! In your driveway or backyard, hang a sheet to use as your screen, set up a projector, and screen his favorite movie from the front seat of your car. Consider buying some typical drive-in fare, such as nachos or burgers, to munch on as you watch!

Buy all of the seats for one show at a small local movie theater, so that the two of you get to enjoy the big screen all by yourselves!

Using your partner's favorite sweet ingredients, take a night to create a brand-new dessert in her honor. Serve it to friends or family the next time you host a dinner party or barbecue.

Plan a trip to a foreign country without telling her, and then take her out for a surprise shopping trip (without telling her why). In her purse, make sure to hide some currency from the country you're going to visit, along with a piece of paper that shows the current exchange rate. Make sure she finds it while you're shopping!

Get a glass etching company to come and engrave a mirror in your home. The engraving can be the lyrics to a song the two of you find special, a quote, an important date, or even just a short and sweet love letter to him.

Take a weekend to go on a photo safari. The two of you should explore a city or town that you've never been to before, taking pictures of yourselves in every location you can. When you get back home, make an album of your adventure.

If your partner is a bird lover, consider buying him a parrot. Parrots are easily trained, and you can teach them to repeat simple phrases, including "I love you." Plus, you can pretend you're on a tropical vacation all year long!

Several companies will make graphical representations of sound waves, like those that are generated when you say, "I love you." Have a piece of art, or just a casual around-the-house T-shirt, made with the visual representation of you expressing your love.

Get thumbprint art made. Many companies will take fingerprints and blow them up so they can be placed on a nice canvas and hung as artwork. Hang both of your fingerprints together to symbolize the bond you share.

If she has a favorite or much-loved product that only comes into season or is only sold once a year, buy her a surprise stockpile so she can enjoy it all year round! If it's a fruit or vegetable, you can pickle or can it so that it lasts for months.

Plant a small sapling in your yard, and then carefully carve your names and a heart into the young tree. Watch your names and the heart grow as the tree grows over the course of months, years, and decades.

Start a fiftieth-anniversary jar to help you look ahead to many loving years together. Each year on your anniversary, put in one object that most fully represents your love for that year—it can be symbolic or literal. After fifty years, open up your collection, and look back on all of the things that have had meaning for you throughout your relationship.

Send her away for a weekend with her friends to a nice little hotel or spa. While she's away, take care of something around the house that's been bothering her—anything from fixing the toilet seat to mowing the yard to repainting a room. If the project is something that she's been meaning to do but hasn't had time, even better!

Take a "rich" day. Test-drive a ridiculously expensive car, buy exorbitantly expensive food and drinks (caviar and high-end champagne are good starts), go to the opera, and generally pamper each other with all the niceties.

If he has a favorite brand of beer or wine, surprise him with a trip to the vineyard or brewery that produces it. Take a tour, and buy enough bottles to last him a whole year!

• • •

Hire an artist to paint or sketch a scene from your wedding or, if you're not married, from a major romantic moment the two of you shared. See if she recognizes what the artist created!

Make a combined family-tree project.
Roots and history are important to
anyone, and by taking the time to
make a real family tree from both
sides of your family, you'll make the
connection between the two of you
that much deeper. You can do this as a
small project or turn it into a full work
of art on display. Better yet, bring
the information to a professional,
and surprise your partner with the
finished tree.

Take a love note that you've written to her (or a meaningful phrase or song lyric) and have a craft shop turn it into a quilt with your words on it. Give it to her to keep her warm inside and out on cold winter nights!

If your partner has a favorite animal at the zoo, arrange for him to have an up-close meet and greet with a zoologist and the animal. There are also a number of interactive animal facilities around the world, meaning you may have to travel to visit the animal's natural habitat.

K eep track of all of her unique sayings, expressions, and idioms, and write them down in a short scrapbook. Present it to her and say, "A dozen tiny reasons why I love you." By noticing the little things, you'll be doing a big thing.

Take him on a
surprise vacation to the country where
his ancestors came from. If he's
Irish, go to Ireland. If he's French, go
to France. If his origins are a mix of
many countries, take multiple trips!

Send old-fashioned
snail-mail letters to her office every
time you come up with a creative or
unique idea for a date. She'll really
begin to look forward to the romantic
break in the work day.

Refurbish or reuse an heirloom from his family. Old china or silverware, for instance, can be refinished, polished, and returned to its former glory. Family heirlooms are a tangible connection to your partner's past.

If she has a favorite artist, book a trip out of town to see that artist's works in person at a museum or traveling exhibit. This can also apply to a musician or stage actor—make a vacation out of going to see a performance in a city that's not your own!

Ask him to tell you about a favorite childhood memory, and then do your best to revisit that experience as grown-ups. You can do many of the same things he did as a child; but instead of simply replicating a childhood memory, add in a bit of grown-up romance.

Arrange to have her shadow or interview a leading figure in whatever subject or field that most interests her. It doesn't have to be the field that she actually works in; it can be anything from architecture to cooking to anything in between.

Hire him a personal assistant for a week, or if you have the funds, for a month. Nothing says "love" like giving your partner the celebrity treatment!

Learn to play her favorite song— on her favorite instrument. If she loves the sound of the cello, and she's a big Madonna fan, well then, you'd better start learning "La Isla Bonita" on the cello!

Start a world-tour album. Make a list of twenty of the most important landmarks in the world. You can use the Wonders of the World list as a starting point, or together you can come up with your own landmarks. Once you've narrowed down the list, make it your mission to take one great picture of the two of you in front of each of those landmarks.

Personalize a board game for him. There are many companies that will create personalized versions of famous games, but to create an extra special game, build it from scratch yourself. Because it is a personal craft project, everything from the dice to the game pieces can have special meaning and symbolism.

Arrange a flashmob in his honor. Take him out for a date in the city, and make sure to have him in the prearranged place at the right time. The flashmob could sing his favorite song or simply dance. Dedicate the performance to your partner.

Buy a week-long subway ad that professes your love. Ideally, the ad will be displayed on the line your partner takes to work. If not, make sure that you come up with an excuse to take her on the specific subway line during the course of the week! Don't make the sign anything embarrassing, though, and don't put too much personal information on it!

*T*ake her to dance lessons so that the two of you learn how to perform her favorite dance. Then, surprise her with tickets to the country where that dance is most prevalent, so the two of you can show off your moves in Argentina, Spain, or . . . Austria!

Run a marathon, a half-marathon, or a triathlon while wearing a shirt with his name on it. If you can qualify for the bigger marathons, even better! You'll probably be shown on a TV for at least a few seconds, so your love will be seen by everyone watching.

In the winter, hire a company to make an ice sculpture of a heart while the two of you are out and about. Have the company leave the sculpture on your front lawn or porch for when you return!

Plant flower seeds in the pattern of a heart or of her initials. As the flowers grow during the course of the year, they will gradually reveal that you planted them in a specific and thoughtful way.

Have a florist buy or create flowers in her favorite color. Many flowers accept color dyes through the soil, and you'd also be surprised by how many different shades of flowers grow naturally. She will find it extra special to receive flowers, especially ones that don't normally grow in her favorite color.

Dedicate a donation in his name to his favorite charity or cause, and then take him to one of the annual galas or fundraisers that the group likely throws. Not only will this allow him to dress up in his black-tie finest, but you'll be making a difference in something that's important to your partner.

Write a joint love note with your partner, then place it in a glass bottle, and close it tightly. Take a trip to the beach (try to do this in the early morning or late at night) and drop the message in a bottle into the ocean, so that your love can travel the world!

Arrange to have a catered meal at her favorite museum or aquarium. Most of these establishments will let you rent out areas for functions after hours. What better way to spend some time at a favorite spot than to make a romantic dinner out of it?

Here's a creative way to do some sightseeing, as long as your partner isn't afraid of heights: Show her an aerial photo of an interesting or beautiful location, and ask her if she'd like to see that view with you. A "yes" answer means that you should literally let her see *that view* by taking her up for a helicopter ride.

Get fortune cookies made for the two of you with specific messages written inside of them. When you go out to eat at a Chinese restaurant, or order takeout, slip them to the waiter, and have them delivered with your meal like a normal fortune cookie. Watch her reaction when she gets the personalized note instead of an obscure fortune!

Send your partner love letters to the home that you both share! He'll be shocked—in a good way—to get letters from the special person he lives with. There's something classically romantic about receiving a love letter in the mail.

• • •

Take her for a short and easy hike; but before you go, set up the destination with a picnic and some romantic gifts as a reward for her efforts. Just make sure not to leave food out if you're hiking in bear country!

Take a shared class on glass blowing, and then use your newfound expertise to create a glass piece (with supervision, of course!) for your home. The piece might not come out perfectly, but every time you walk by it, you'll remember that you did it together.

Take a trip to Europe, and do your best to eat breakfast and dinner in two separate countries! With the quality railway system that runs between most European countries, this isn't as hard to do as it sounds—and it's quite an accomplishment!

This is a broad but meaningful idea: Find out your partner's greatest regret in life, and see what you can do to help him correct it. It's never too late to go back to school, change careers, heal a strained family relationship, or do any number of things. Having support for an endeavor like this is truly meaningful.

Make up a simple code that uses the letters of his name as the cipher that unlocks the text (there are websites that can help you design codes like this). Once you've created it, use your new code to send him romantic messages that no one else will be able to understand!

Plan a desserts-only dinner that consists of all of his favorite sweet treats. Make sure there's a variety of dessert options to keep him on his toes! A little fruit goes a long way to break up an excess of chocolate.

Throughout the day, send your partner two dozen subtle hints on her phone about where you're going to take her that night for a date. See how long it takes her to guess where you're going!

Buy him season tickets to his favorite sporting event or pastime, and when he goes for the first time, pay an attendant a few dollars to bring him a special piece of memorabilia that you've already bought for him—a signed baseball, a jersey, or something similar.

Have a color-centric meal. Plan and cook a special meal that consists of different sorts of food that all share your partner's favorite color(s). While you can cheat and use food coloring, try to be creative and actually source food that is the correct color. You'll be able to find most any color if you look for it—there are even items like Peruvian purple potatoes that can help you out!

*B*uy a small portable radio, and use it to send a message of your love out over the airwaves. If you want to go for even stronger symbolism, aim your message out into space so that the whole universe knows how you feel! Record the message that you send, and then play it back for her.

Go to a local diner or small, independent sandwich shop and ask them to name a sandwich or a dish after your partner. If you can come up with a really unique combination of ingredients, they might bestow the name to you! Then take your partner to the restaurant to reveal this gesture of love.

Record a nice, heartfelt, and sweet video about your love in secret, and then upload it to his video library on his smartphone or laptop. Send him some hints through the day that will gently guide him to where the video is stored.

Send her a *series* of love notes, each of which contains one extra *single* letter of the alphabet at the end of the note. Send one note per day, and after *she* has received all of the notes, have her try to unscramble the extra alphabet letters to reveal an additional, hidden message.

If you know that he is going to be having a stressful day at work, call and order lunch from his favorite restaurant to be delivered to him at his office. Consider also calling a florist to bring by some flowers to accompany lunch.

· · ·

Bring her to an author signing of her favorite writer. This can be a local or distant location, depending on the author's tour schedules. While there, make sure to buy her a copy of the author's book (or books) so that it can be signed.

Take him to a restaurant operated by his favorite celebrity chef, and then surprise him with tickets to an upcoming taping of that chef's TV show. If the favorite chef doesn't host a live audience, then get tickets to a show by another, similar chef who does.

Buy a handheld video camera, and film your entire day together on a weekend when you don't have any special plans. Edit the footage, and then turn it into a short, touching film that highlights all the ways the two of you show love on any given day.

Access her contacts list in her phone, and then change your name as it currently appears. Also, alter the ringtone that comes up when you call. You should change your name to a sweet compliment, and make the new ringtone a romantic song or a song with special meaning to both of you. When you call her she will see a love message from you to her, accompanied by the song that you chose.

Take a dance class, and then stage your own flashmob in the middle of a crowded area where you can show off your dancing chops and your connection to each other. If that's too nerve-wracking, then just choreograph your own dance to do at home with no one watching but him!

Buy a handkerchief and have it monogrammed with both of your initials or with a secret acronym that only has meaning to the two of you. You could also trade handkerchiefs so each of you has a secret message from the other.

When you go out of town for work or for leisure, leave a hidden surprise behind at home to brighten your partner's day when he finds it. If he doesn't call you to tell you about this surprise by the time the trip is winding down, give him a hint!

Hire a waiter to class up an otherwise normal dinner date for the two of you at home. Grill some basic barbecue food (or even order takeout), and then enjoy the pleasures of a simple meal delivered with great service.

Splurge, and spoil him by getting something out of season or out of the area flown in for him. Get a lobster from Boston, blueberries from Maine, or a real Georgia peach! Keep overseas treats in mind, too!

Switch up tradition by going for a nice walk and picnic at night, instead of during the day. Nighttime takes the romance of a picnic in the park and ramps it up significantly. Make sure it's a moonlit night, and bring bug spray in case the mosquitoes are out.

Give a gift within a gift. Surprise her with a nice, framed photo of the two of you to place on her desk or around the home. Behind the photo, hide two tickets to a concert, a festival, or some other event that she has been wanting to attend. Attach a small sticky note to the frame of the picture that lets her know to check behind the photo.

Make a special day that the two of you agree to celebrate as a holiday every year. It can be a completely random date or it can be a date that has a deeper meaning for your relationship. In either case, make sure to get presents, a cake, and write a heartfelt card for this "holiday" each year.

*M*ake a "rain date." Take advantage of the next stretch of bad weather by buying some matching rain boots, and then go outside to kiss and play in the rain. If you'd rather chase the rain than wait for it to come to you, how about scheduling a trip to Seattle or some other famously rainy location?

Instead of having breakfast in bed, have a whole lazy day together. Don't leave the bedroom, except to make breakfast, lunch, and dinner together, and then enjoy your meals in bed. Just make sure to watch out for crumbs in the blankets.

Create your own impromptu scavenger hunt in a bookstore. Hide little love notes to your partner in books that have special meaning to him (a favorite book, a travel guide to your honeymoon location, for example), and give him hints to help him find all of the notes!

*T*rade deep secrets. Set aside a day for the two of you to tell each other a secret that you've never told anyone before. The secrets don't have to be dark or disturbing, just something private. Being a secret keeper for your partner is a great way to increase your intimacy.

Crash a wedding and pretend that it's yours. Don't be rude, don't be annoying, just slink into a large wedding and relive (or imagine) it as your wedding. Get out on the dance floor and enjoy each other's company, along with the atmosphere of love that weddings bring.

*T*ake a hot-air balloon ride over a pastoral country setting, and take pictures from the air. Back on the ground, make it a quest to reach all of the places you photographed. Have a picnic on as many of those spots as you can.

Buy him new work clothes (with his input, unless you're very good at choosing), and take the time to stitch a small heart somewhere secret on each piece of clothing. It will let him know that you're thinking about him all day.

If she has a favorite flower, preferably an exotic flower, take a trip to the country that produces those flowers. And no, greenhouses don't count! Buy her a big bouquet of flowers while you're there, and they will be the most memorable flowers she's ever received.

• • •

Take a vacation together to a national park or parks, and take a moment to plant a seed while you're there. Every year, take a brief vacation to visit your plant and see how it's growing.

Take the classic American road trip—with a twist. Fly to another city, rent a car for a week, and then drive as far as you can before coming back when the week is up. Stay at any inns or hotels that catch your fancy, and don't be afraid to stop and chat with the locals.

Tease her with a reverse-developing present. On the first day, leave out a wrapping bow, with no note or explanation. On the second day, leave a box, wrapped with a bow, but with nothing inside of it. On the last day, leave your present in the wrapped box. Make sure that the present is worth the wait, though!

On the anniversary of when you first met, take the day off and recreate the way in which you were first introduced. If you can't recreate what you did that day, at least travel to the location where you met and surprise your partner by giving him an updated version of the first gift you ever gave him.

If you're already married, have a jeweler create a totally unique, brand-new anniversary band to mark the occasion of your marriage. If you're not married, ask the jeweler to design and craft a one-of-a-kind necklace or bracelet. The piece doesn't have to be studded with diamonds; it just has to be unique.

When he leaves for work in the morning, follow him there, but stay out of sight. Before you head out, send him an e-mail that says, "Look outside," so when he logs on to his computer, he'll see the message. Be waiting outside with flowers.

Go on a trip to see her favorite style of music performed in the area where it originated. If she likes the blues, for example, take a music-themed trip down the Mississippi to visit some of the famous blues locales along the route.

Pay to post a Google ad about your partner that will respond to a specific phrase that you know she searches with some regularity. When she types that search term in, she'll see a banner ad that tells her how much you care about her.

Set up a geocaching challenge for the two of you, but make sure that the caches are all marked with romantic objects or items that have special meaning or significance to the two of you and your relationship.

If you're going out of town, buy an alarm clock that can be programmed to play a certain song for your partner. Make sure he wakes up to "your song" or to a song that has special meaning for the two of you.

Turn one wall of your kitchen into a love-notes blackboard. There are several types of spray paint that will turn any surface into a blackboard. Once the board is dry, use it to leave her love notes in the morning or during the day.

Take her fishing, with a catch: Have the lines set up before you get to the location, and attach her line to a watertight bag that contains a piece of jewelry for her. Make sure it's strongly attached so that it doesn't come loose as she's reeling it in!

Contact your local ice-skating rink, and arrange for them to allow the two of you in for a special, private skating session. Put your smartphone, or other portable media player (or use the PA system), in the seats and play romantic music that sets the tone for the two of you.

Turn your partner's car into a scavenger hunt. Hide small romantic notes or gifts around the inside of her car without telling her. When she next opens the glove compartment or the center console, she'll see the thoughtful present that you've left for her. Other good hiding spots include the seatback pockets, underneath the seats, and above the sun visor.

If he's a big fan of a certain TV show, rent all of the seasons of the show on DVD. Then set aside a weekend to lie around on the couch together and take in the episodes. Bonus points for making food and drinks that are related in some way to the content or setting of the show.

If she likes the outdoors, consider surprising her with a brand-new bike so that the two of you can ride together. Make sure you get her measurements first so that the store can help you select the best bicycle for her size.

Make him coffee, the hard way. Book a trip for the two of you to the location that grows his favorite variety of coffee, like Costa Rica, Jamaica, Guatemala, or any of several others. Bring back as much unground coffee beans as you can, and then make his coffee with it each morning!

Hire a private chef to come and make one exceptional meal for the two of you on a special anniversary. You'll get all of the benefits of going to a great restaurant without dealing with traffic or waiting for a table.

Hide a piece of jewelry inside a dessert that you've baked or crafted especially for her. However, be very careful that she doesn't eat the jewelry by accident—that would pretty well ruin the mood of the moment!

Go antiquing together, and splurge by buying her something that she really loves but would never get for herself. If she's a history buff, make sure that the piece you're buying has an interesting and varied history that will enthrall her.

Surprise him by changing his computer desktop or laptop wallpaper to a picture of you holding up a sign that tells him how much you love him. Alternatively, the picture can be of a special surprise that you bought for him, or it can be sentimental—a picture of your honeymoon location, perhaps.

In a more literal way, relive your honeymoon by booking a quick getaway to the same place that you stayed after you got married. If you're not yet married, but have taken a vacation together, take another short getaway to that vacation spot!

Recreate (or imagine in advance) your honeymoon. Break out your photo albums, cook dishes indigenous to your vacation spot, and listen to music that captures the spirit of being there. Give him a quiz about memorable moments that occurred during your honeymoon (not too hard), with a prize of your choosing when he gets the answers right!

Give each other cards without buying them. Take a trip to the store and trade romantic cards with each other without purchasing them. You can choose cards for any occasion; just make sure the sentiments are right.

Make wilderness food indoors! On a cold winter night, light a fire in your fireplace, and grill steaks and burgers over it. It's a night that promises all the fun of camping but without the freezing temperatures.

Develop a special, heartfelt drinking toast that can become your standard toast for the two of you. Say it whenever you're at a restaurant together or enjoying wine or cocktails at home. If you want to be sneaky, you can also quietly add it on to the end of any other toasts the two of you are involved in—just be sure not to upstage the actual toast!

Call a radio station and request a song to be played for your partner. You can take this classic move a step further by phoning in to a local radio station while the two of you are on vacation away from home! Your partner will really appreciate the added effort you put into this special request.

If he's a true child at heart, either build or enlist someone to build a romantic tree house for the two of you. You can keep it stocked with adult snacks like wine and baguettes, and the two of you can retreat to the tree house whenever the urge strikes you!

Make her a special chair that she can always sit in when she wants to read or watch TV. Classic, wooden chairs with beautiful details are a timeless and romantic piece of furniture, but make sure you know what you're doing so that you don't end up with a broken chair and an angry partner.

Take an afternoon to help him build a
life list of all of the important things
he'd like to be, do, see, and accomplish.
Supporting him as he dreams and plans
for his ideal future is a true show of
love. Once the list is made, keep it in
a safe place, and reference it often to
make sure you're doing all that you can
to help him achieve these longstanding
goals and dreams.

ring her to a water fountain, and give her a whole bag of pennies that you've saved so that she can make as many wishes as she can think of. If you want, ask her to pick one wish and tell it to you out loud, and then do everything in your power to make that wish come true.

Go on a building tour. If your partner is an architecture or design buff, consider visiting one of the classic architecture cities like Boston, Chicago, New York, or Washington, D.C., to give him a taste of the variety of fascinating buildings those cities contain. Contact the local architectural society before you go, and arrange for someone to give you a walking tour, pointing out the highlights as you go.

Take a large truck (either your own or borrowed from a friend or relative) out of the city and to the country, away from as much light pollution as possible. Lay down a few sleeping bags in the truck bed, then lie back and take in the night sky. When you get cold or uncomfortable, you can just head back!

Buy her favorite music on old-fashioned albums, and then buy her a record player so that she can listen to them. There's something incredibly romantic about the classic record player.

If your partner has a favorite tropical destination, help him relive the memories of that place by downloading sounds of its native birds and animals. Use the environmental sounds as a backdrop to help you think up new places to explore together.

Have a nineteenth-century throwback date. Try to keep your romantic outing confined to only those things that existed in the 1800s. For example, stay away from artificial light and walk (or ride horses) everywhere. And if you're looking to eat out, see if you can find a really old-fashioned general store. No trendy nightclubs for you!

There's no better way to see the country than traveling by train. Surprise her with two roundtrip tickets for a train tour of the heartlands. You'll see incredible scenery, and you won't have to worry about driving. Plus, nothing compares to the classic luxury of a train voyage for real romance.

Set up a miniature golf course inside your own home. Nothing beats the playfulness of taking someone completely by surprise, as this is bound to do. You can use Wiffle golf balls if you're worried about breaking anything. As alternatives, consider an indoor beanbag toss or indoor bowling. Just make sure you let him win, and reward him justly when he does!

*S*urprise her by buying her a full outfit for a night out on the town. The outfit should be everything from undergarments (your choice!) to clothes, from shoes to accessories. Make sure she looks appropriate for where you're taking her on the date!

Make a totally unexpected piece of "art" for him. Carve an amorous message into a fruit or a vegetable. In the fall, this could be a pumpkin; and in the summer, you could use a watermelon, for example. Be creative! Plus, after you deliver your message of love, the two of you can enjoy the pumpkin or watermelon.

Have a teenage date day. Hit up the mall's food court for some fun, but decidedly not gourmet, food, and then head for the arcade or miniature golf course. After that, schedule in some time for a late-night movie, and then spend some time cruising the empty roads late at night—it's a great time to just open up and talk to each other.

Before your partner goes away on a business trip, mail a small card and present to the hotel where he'll be staying. Mail them out far enough in advance so that they are waiting for him when he arrives to check in.

• • •

To surprise her with an upcoming beach vacation, hide all of her shoes (on a weekend, of course) and replace them with sandals. Sprinkle some sand around for added effect, but make sure to vacuum up afterward.

ooperate on a finger painting. Let her dip your fingers
into the paint, and then allow her
to control your arms and use you
to make designs. You'd better trust
her if you're going to do this—one
wrong move could leave you covered in paint!

A small and simple idea, but a good one: Order supplies for your partner's home office that have his name printed on them— pens, paper, business cards, etc. Present these supplies in a nice package with a heartfelt, handwritten note that tells him how you feel about him!

Surprise her by renting a photo booth (like the kind that you'd find in the mall). The two of you can have a fun evening taking pictures in it. If the feeling strikes you, you could always get a bit risqué in the booth. After all, you rented it, so you should be able to do what you want . . . within reason, of course! After you take the shots, leave them around with little notes telling her that you love her.

Go for a classic country drive—
on the other side of the country!
If you live on the East Coast, fly
to California, rent a convertible,
and cruise Route 1 up and down
the coast. If you live out West, fly
to Florida and drive through the
Florida Keys. If you live up North,
consider hitting up the Southwest
for historic Route 66 and some
desert scenery. Convertibles are
the classic cars to go with here!

If your partner has a rough commute to work, hire a private driver for her for a week, or for one day a week for a month. Encourage her to use the time in the car to relax and unwind.

Make each other good luck charms to carry on a daily basis. They can be simple and silly, but if you make them for each other, they'll have meaning. Seal them with a kiss!

The next time he travels for work, send a mysterious note to his destination that will be waiting for him when he arrives. Make sure it's a cryptic note, but one that is clearly from you. Give him hints as to how much you've been missing him, and that you don't feel like you can wait until he gets back home to be with him. Then book a flight, and follow him out to his destination. Greet him at his hotel or motel with wine, snacks, and amorous attention!

Spend some time pulling together a list of why you love her. Then, bring the list to a professional letterpress shop, and have them emboss it or print it with a high-quality finish so that it becomes a keepsake. Surprise your partner with it at the end of a long day and watch it instantly brighten her mood!

Adapt the idea of a message in a bottle to the bathroom! Write a short note and place it in a small glass bubble; then fill up the bathtub for her, letting her find the note on her own. The note can be serious or sexy, depending on your mood and on what you think she'd appreciate. After all, some people don't want to do anything but relax in the tub!

*C*reate a boardwalk in your backyard! Rent a popcorn machine, a cotton candy machine, and hire a juggler or a caricature artist to come and entertain the two of you. Have corn dogs, nachos, and other carnival-esque foods; and don't forget the slushies!

Recreate the teenage "makeout spot." Drive your car to a secluded location, put on some music from the era he was in high school, and try to remember what it was like to be young and in love.

• • •

If you build a driveway, set a mailbox, or do anything that requires concrete, put both of your names in it before it fully sets so that you'll always be able to look at your names together and smile.

*L*earn calligraphy so that you can write exceptional hand-written notes to him. Nothing says old-world romance like a nicely, artistically rendered love note; and there's no better way to produce one of those than to get a lovely calligraphy set and start practicing! Plus, you'll find that your new-found skills come in handy, such as when addressing envelopes for formal parties or for other similar occasions.

Make scented aromatherapy candles for her using her favorite smells. You can find instructions for how to do this online, or you can look up any of the numerous businesses that will create custom candles for you, based on your instructions and input. Having a scented candle to relax her at the end of a long day, especially one that you took the time to think about and create just for her, will be priceless.

Leave secret notes for him on the bathroom mirror. Use the corner of a bar of soap to gently write out a love message on the mirror. You won't be able to see the message under normal conditions, but the next time he takes a shower, the soap will repel steam from those areas that it touched, so your message will be clearly visible in the steamed-up mirror when he gets out of the shower.

If she enjoys birdwatching, surprise her with a trip to a premier birdwatching location and a brand-new pair of high-end binoculars. Because birds vary so widely by location, take her somewhere outside of your local area to give her the opportunity to see as many different types of birds as possible!

Treat her like royalty by buying her a brand-new outfit for a night out on the town. Tell her to meet you at a hotel in the city, and have the concierge bring the new outfit to the hotel room for her. Then, hit the town!

• • •

Every day for a week, pick a different, totally unique spot for a brief rendezvous during lunch or after work. Don't tell him where the spot is until just before it's time for him to go there. Greet him with a kiss!

Turn a closet into a romantic storage shelf. Clear out a small coat closet, add lights, and remove the door so that he can see inside it. Then, add some shelving, and layer the shelving with meaningful books, crafts, letters, and other memorabilia that the two of you have collected over the course of your relationship. Every time you come across something new and meaningful, add it to the shelf and watch your collection grow.

Invent a breakfast "combo meal" and name it after him. Take your cue here from places like IHOP or Denny's, where they give unique names to their various combinations of pancakes, eggs, and sausages. Surprise him with a breakfast that's composed of all of his favorite foods, and tell him that from now on, that combination will be named after him!

Play travel darts. When he comes home, quickly blindfold him, and lead him to just in front of a map of the world that you've pasted on a dartboard. Still blindfolded, give him a dart and tell him to walk forward and stick it into the dartboard. If he has trouble finding the dartboard, help him out, but don't guide his exact choice. Once he's placed the dart, take off the blindfold, and he'll see where you're going to take him on your next vacation.

Make an organizational pin board for all of her materials (keys, tools, etc.) This is especially nice if she is prone to losing or forgetting anything on a frequent basis. Inscribe the board with a loving message to her. Plans for this sort of board vary widely—a quick search online will show you what sort of organizational board best suits your space needs.

While your partner is at work, hire an artist to create a chalk design in your driveway professing your love for her. If you're confident in your own skills with artistry, you can take this on yourself!

If your partner has a big presentation at work or some sort of milestone at her job, fill her car up with balloons during the day, and place a heartfelt congratulations card from you on her seat.

*J*f he drives a good amount, surprise him by taking his car to get detailed. You'd be shocked how much of a difference a nice, clean car makes for someone who has to spend a lot of time driving. If you really want to go above and beyond, have the car repainted and given a full enhancement package to make it shine like new.

Go to a ring-making class or jewelry-making class together, and design matching pieces that you both can wear on a daily basis. The pieces you make don't have to be expensive or fancy; just knowing that you're connected through something you designed and made together is a great way to feel closer to each other.

Go on a safari. Safaris combine the fun of travel with a healthy dose of adventure—and they're an incredible bonding experience. Safaris cost more than many other types of vacations, so you might have to forego one or two smaller trips in order to finance it, but the experiences it provides will be worth it. Sleeping under the stars after a day of tracking beautiful, wild animals is truly one of the most transformative experiences you can have as a couple.

Grow a flower garden specifically so that you can make homemade bouquets for her at a moment's notice. Grow flowers that pair together well, and think about adding some complementary greenery to set off the color of the flowers. Once the plants have started to grow in, harvest a few flowers each week and hand-deliver the bouquet to her with a love note attached!

Go to a classy bar and have the bartender create and name a new drink after her. Not only will you be able to recreate it at home, but it will have the prestige of coming from a swanky location.

Take the time to clean and remodel his home office when he leaves for a business trip. Get him a brand-new chair (unless he really loves the one he has), nice lamps, and a classy rug. Top it all off with a picture of the two of you.

Buy him a small, easy-to-care-for pet, such as a betta fish. Note: Don't do this if he doesn't like animals! In general, a small animal like a fish doesn't take the commitment that a dog or a cat does, but it's still a cute way to say that you love him. If you want to surprise him with a dog or a cat, bonus points for that, but keep in mind that you'll have to train a puppy or a kitten, and you will need to work your lifestyle around walks and feedings!

If you want to remind her of a special place that the two of you have shared, whether it's a honeymoon location or a park where you had your first kiss, keep a constant reminder of it by filling a small glass vial with sand or soil from that spot. If these spots are overseas, it may be difficult to obtain this sort of keepsake. However, there are several companies that do sell dirt from Ireland and other notable destinations, for example. You can also be creative and get in touch with locals to help you, and then figure out ways to have them ship it to you.

Choose a famous foreign book to read together—anything from a children's novel to a romance to a pulp thriller. The main criterion is to select a book that is prominently set in some exotic location. Once you finish reading the book together, book a trip to visit the country where it was set!

Play a game to see how well you know each other. Go to the mall and give yourselves $20 each. Select a spot to meet after thirty minutes of shopping, and then separate. The game is to find the "best" gift you can for your partner within the budget and timeframe allowed. No cheating. Neither of you is allowed to buy something that the other already has. Each gift should be a totally new item. The gifts in this game can be quirky and offbeat, as long as the receiver appreciates it!

Put on a fireworks display for him. Contact a pyro-technic company and find out what it would cost to put on a small display for your partner. This show can be used to celebrate an anniversary, some special achievement, or just be-cause! Make sure you have an appropriate location from which to launch the fireworks, however.

*P*ack her a special bag filled with all of her favorite candies, and sneak it into her briefcase when she heads to work or goes away on a business trip. Nothing sweetens up the day like candy, and no candy is quite as sweet as candy that comes as a surprise!

Make some random, common object "your" object (similar to having a song that's "your" song). It can be something totally innocuous, such as oak leaves, or dandelions, or even something man-made like binder clips. It sounds silly, but it's an easy way to show your partner you're thinking about him when you leave "your" object around for him to find.

Contact her boss, and ask for permission to come into the office after hours to decorate her workspace as a surprise. You can either decorate it tactfully, with little items placed around, or if she's not the type to get embarrassed, you can really go big with balloons, streamers, and everything that goes along with a full-scale party.

The next time you go to the beach, bury a small gift in the sand while he is in the water or napping. Leave a treasure map with him as you go down to the ocean, giving him time to find it before you return.

If he's a fan of Shakespeare, or of the theater in general, deliver a soliloquy to him in the character of a Shakespearean actor, complete with props. Open the props to reveal two tickets to a Shakespearean festival—in London.

Get a computer-savvy
or programming-savvy
friend to help you write some
basic software that will display
love messages on your partner's
computer when he does certain
actions. Make sure, though,
that it's not interfering with any
important functions or any work
that he needs to get done.

Take a trip to see the stars. The night sky is possibly the most romantic view that we have here on Earth; but even in the countryside, we still usually miss out on its full beauty. To really get a full appreciation of the night sky, take her to a certified dark-sky area (search online for locations near where you live). In these spots, no outside light at all pollutes the view of the sky, and the stars will be well beyond anything you've seen previously.

Call a store where she's a regular (and where she will be recognized by the staff). Arrange for the store staff to hold a special present for the next time she shops at that store, and have them surprise her with it when she arrives. This works best at small craft stores, antique shops, or any local stores that have a staff that will recognize your partner and be willing to accommodate your request.

Take him to flying lessons!
If he's always wanted to soar, taking some lessons in a small, nimble Cessna or other aircraft is a great way to learn new things and to experience the freedom and exhilaration that comes with flight. Of course, if he's afraid of flying or of heights, this probably isn't the best idea. But for those who enjoy flying, flight lessons are truly a marvelous gift.

Ask her to meet you for dinner at a predetermined location—it can be anywhere of your choosing. You'll then need to enlist the help of eleven friends of yours or hers. Give each friend a single rose and a small note. They should approach her at the restaurant and give her the rose and the note. Make sure that they approach her one at a time, over the span of a few minutes. Once all of the roses have been delivered, except for the last one in the dozen, bring the rose to her yourself!

If your man is a big racing fan (or just loves driving fast), a wonderful gift would be a day-long racing experience with a real NASCAR vehicle. These experiences are offered in several locations. Generally, there's a brief classroom portion at the beginning of the day, and then the participants get to experience the speed, both as a passenger in the car and as the driver!

Find out her absolute favorite meal from childhood, and recreate it for her without warning. If needed, you can consult her parents to find out exactly how they used to prepare the dish.

• • •

Hide a set of three to five small gifts throughout your home, with each gift containing a clue to the location of the next one. Don't let him cheat or find the clues out of order!

Plant her favorite type of fruit tree in your yard so that she can have her favorite fresh fruit every time it is in season! If the fruit absolutely won't grow in your climate, then you'll have to improvise and be creative. Find out if there are any other fruits that are very similar that will work. Or, discover if there are any greenhouses in your area that might let you take some of the fruit if you contribute to the upkeep of the tree.

Corny, but classic: Make him lunch for work, and cut everything into the shape of a heart! Sandwiches are the easiest food to do this with (you probably wouldn't want to try it with pasta, for instance!), and you can also send a heart-shaped cookie, heart-shaped pineapple slices, heart-shaped rice cakes, or anything else that's carvable and will last until lunchtime!

Mark the next full moon or harvest moon by waking her up to have a nighttime champagne toast and chocolate-dipped strawberries. This works much better on a weekend, so try to plan accordingly!

If she enjoys spending some time outdoors, especially by firelight, surprise her and build a fire pit outside of your home where the two of you can sit and relax. Make it more unique by carving her name into the cement you pour.

Buy a postcard or postcards from a famous monument or destination, gift-wrap them, and then give them to your partner, with a note that says: "You'll be needing these." Then reveal to her that you've booked a trip for the two of you to visit the landmark. The postcards are so she doesn't have to buy them when you're on vacation —she can get a head start on writing them before you leave!

If he gets sick, give him a special, extra-romantic box of tissues! Cover the box with love notes, and, if you're feeling really inspired, take the tissues out, draw a little heart on each one, and then put them back into the box before he uses them. Sure, they'll get thrown away, but the fact that you went to the trouble of decorating them just so that he'd feel a little bit better is bound to make him as happy as he can be while he's sick!

Buy a box of her favorite cereal, open up the box (but not the inner cereal bag), and then put your own version of a cereal-box prize inside! Instead of a decoder ring or a kaleidoscope, though, fill your box with romantic gifts, such as jewelry, and make sure to include a nice note! The last step is the most important: Seal the box back up with a little bit of glue so that she'll be completely surprised when she opens the "new" box and finds a surprise waiting for her inside!

Give your dishware and dishwasher a rest: buy a stack of paper plates for your meals. Before each meal, write a special note on the edge or on the underside of the plate, and set the plate down so that he can see what you've written! Make sure, though, not to use ink that soaks through the plate, and make sure to keep the food off of the areas where you've written!